Surviving Last Period on Fridays and Other Desperate Situations

Cottonwood Game Book for Language Arts

(formerly published as *Cottonwood Game Book*)

Cheryl Miller Thurston

Cottonwood Press, Inc.
Fort Collins, Colorado

Requests for permission, other than personal classroom use, should be addressed to:

Cottonwood Press, Inc.
109-B Cameron Drive
Fort Collins, CO 80525

800-864-4297

www.cottonwoodpress.com

ISBN 1-877673-01-3

Printed in the United States of America

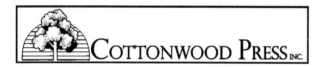

Table of Contents

Using the Book 5

Pass-Back Stories 7

Dictionary Puzzle #1 8

    Answer Key, Dictionary Puzzle #1 10

Dictionary Puzzle #2 11

    Answer Key, Dictionary Puzzle #2 12

Word Chains 13

    Answer Key, Word Chains 14

Alphabet Story 15

    Answer Key, Alphabet Story 16

Alliteration 17

    Answer Key, Alliteration 18

Similes 19

    Answer Key, Similes 20

Hearts 21

    Answer Key, Hearts 22

Newspaper Scavenger Hunt 23

Newspaper Scavenger Hunt List 25

Animals 27

    Answer Key, Animals 28

Spring 29

    Answer Key, Spring 30

Categories 31

Getting Acquainted 33

Goblin 34

    Answer Key, Goblin 35

Antonyms 36

    Answer Key, Antonyms 37

Build a Sentence #1 38

    Answer Key, Build a Sentence #1 39

Build a Sentence #2 40

    Answer Key, Build a Sentence #2 41

Tongue Twisters 42

    Answer Key, Tongue Twisters.....................................43

Letter Pairs..44

    Answer Key, Letter Pairs 45

The Race Is On! 46

    Answer Key, The Race Is On! 47

Shamrocks 48

    Answer Key, Shamrocks 49

Life and Death 50

Tinsel 51

    Answer Key, Tinsel 52

Dear Edna 53

Holiday Challenge 54

Holiday Challenge List 55

    Answer Key, Holiday Challenge 58

Crazy Sentences 59

Rhyming Conversation 60

    Answer Key, Rhyming Conversation 61

Space Race 62

Saying What You Mean 64

Using This Book

You know the feeling. It's school picture day, Halloween costume day or the day before Christmas vacation. The students are acting as if they each had six cups of coffee and a bowl of sugar for breakfast. You find yourself imagining the possibilities of hypnotism and duct tape as teaching aids.

You're not serious, of course — or perhaps only half serious. But you do recognize that today is definitely not the best day to introduce participle phrases.

Now you can turn to *Surviving Last Period on Fridays and Other Desperate Situations* for help. This book is full of language arts games and activities designed especially to interest junior high/middle school students. The games are interesting and challenging — never busy work.

And best of all, they should make life easier for you, the teacher.

Two Types of Activities

There are two types of activities in *Surviving Last Period on Fridays and Other Desperate Situations:*

- Activities that you can photocopy for your own personal classroom use and pass out to your students. These activities have a place for the student's name at the top and directions for the student on the page itself.
- Activities that need some advance preparation, usually minimal. These activities have instructions for you, the teacher.

Many Uses

You will find yourself using *Surviving Last Period on Fridays and Other Desperate Situations* in many situations:

- When the lesson you had planned for the whole period takes just six and a half minutes.
- When you're sure your mind will turn to oatmeal if you have to spend one more day going over capitalization rules.
- When you want to keep the students busy on something interesting while you grade papers or give a student special help — or wait for two aspirin to take effect.
- When the students have just returned from an assembly where a magician sawed two people in half and pulled a boa constrictor out of his sock — and now settling everyone down for some serious spelling work seems less-than-inspired. And probably impossible.
- When you want the students to think, to have some fun with words, to see that language can be fun!

Pass-Back Stories

This game lets students use their creativity, usually keeping them interested for an entire class period.

Materials

- A timer (or a clock with a minute-hand).
- Notebook paper for everyone in class.

Organization

Arrange the room so that students are sitting in equal rows of four or five students each. Have each student put his or her name on a sheet of notebook paper.

Write the beginning of a story on the board and have the students copy it onto their papers. One of these lines usually works well:

- It was a dark and stormy night.
- I couldn't believe my eyes when . . .
- Suddenly, the principal's voice boomed over the intercom.

Instructions

Explain that the line the students have written is the beginning of a story, a story which they are to complete. However, they are not to complete it in a typical manner. Instead, they are to begin writing, working on their stories for only four minutes. When the timer sounds, they must stop writing, even if they are in the middle of a sentence, and pass their papers to the person behind them.

The students must then read the stories they have just been given and continue them, writing for an additional four minutes. (As the stories get longer, it is a good idea to lengthen the writing time to four and a half to five minutes.) The pass-back stories continue, with each successive person adding onto what others have written, until everyone gets his or her original paper back. That person then completes the story, bringing the action to an end.

After the writing is completed, have the students in each row meet as a group to reread the completed stories and to choose the one they like best. Then collect all the chosen stories and read them aloud for everyone.

Suggestions

It is a good idea to mention that everything written should be appropriate for sharing in class — in other words, no profanity, inappropriate subjects, insults, etc. Encourage the students to have fun but to use good judgment at the same time.

Dictionary Puzzle #1

1. Put the following in alphabetical order: *fiddlestick, fiddlefooted, fiddlefaddle, fiddlehead, fiddleback.* _____

   _____

2. Can you store iced tea in a *colander*? Why or why not? _____

   _____

3. Where on a horse's body would you find a *fetlock*? _____
   The *withers*? _____
   The *flank*? _____

4. What is the difference between a *lagoon* and a *legume*? _____

   _____

5. What do *marjoram* and *thyme* have in common? _____

6. Place each of the words listed below into one of the three categories: Jobs, Things to Eat or Types of Homes.

   haddock, lasagna, barrister, kale, kennel, obstetrician, chalet, hovel, podiatrist

Jobs	Things to Eat	Types of Homes

7. Find three animals and three birds that begin with the letter c and have at least five letters.

   Animals

   C _____

   C _____

   C _____

   Birds

   C _____

   C _____

   C _____

8. Would you like to go to a party and commit a *gaffe*? Why or why not? _____

   _____

9. If you were seriously ill, would you want to go to a *charlatan* for treatment? Why or why not? _____

_____

10. Which would you use to help a baby go to sleep, a *berceuse* or a *belladonna*? _____

_____

11. Alphabetically, which word comes in the middle: *puzzle, pachyderm, education, burglar* or *cluster*? _____

12. Would a *lummox* make a good ballet dancer? Why or why not? _____

_____

_____

13. Now write three dictionary questions of your own in the space below:

Question: _____

_____

Answer: _____

_____

Question: _____

_____

Answer: _____

_____

Question: _____

_____

Answer: _____

_____

Answer Key
Dictionary Puzzle #1

1. Fiddleback, fiddlefaddle, fiddlefooted, fiddlehead, fiddlestick.

2. No, because a colander has holes in it.

3. A fetlock is on the back of the leg, above the hoof. The withers are between the shoulder bones. The flank is on the side, between the ribs and the hip.

4. A lagoon is a pond. A legume is a bean or a pea.

5. They are both types of spices used in seasoning.

6.

Jobs	Things to Eat	Types of Homes
Obstetrician	Haddock	Kennel
Podiatrist	Lasagna	Chalet
Barrister	Kale	Hovel

7. Answers will vary. Some possible animals: collie, cheetah, chimpanzee. Some possible birds: crane, cardinal, cormorant.

8. No, because a gaffe is a social blunder.

9. No, because a charlatan pretends to have knowledge or ability he or she lacks.

10. A berceuse, which is a lullaby.

11. Education.

12. No, because a lummox is a clumsy person.

13. Answers will vary.

Name _____

Dictionary Puzzle #2

1. Put the following words into alphabetical order: *scuff, basket, program, cocoa, pinafore, diary, dynamite, domino, dwarf, kidnap, scrap, pillow, ditto, guard, inflate, frail.*

   _____

   _____

   _____

2. What is the plural of *alga*? _____

3. Alphabetically, which comes first, the *chicken* or the *egg*? _____

4. Which word doesn't belong in this list: *lemming, loess, lemur, llama, leopard?* Why? _____

   _____

5. Alphabetically, which of these words comes last: *toxic, spooky, sponge* or *tarpoon?* _____

   _____

6. What do the following words all have in common: *silicon, cobalt, boron, radon, argon, bromine* and *tellurium?* _____

   _____

7. Name five different things that can be called *frog.*

   • _____   • _____

   • _____   • _____

   • _____

8. Could a *hansom* be *handsome?* Why or why not? _____

   _____

True/False

_____ 9. A *wombat* is used for cleaning silverware.

_____10. An *eyelet* is a very small eye.

_____11. A *kismet* is a garden vegetable similar to a squash.

_____12. A *flamenco* is the name of a beautiful pink bird.

_____13. A *bunker* is someone who bunks.

_____14. Most people would like to marry a *reprobate.*

_____15. A *lexicon* would help you answer the questions on this page.

Answer Key
Dictionary Puzzle #2

1. Basket, cocoa, diary, ditto, domino, dwarf, dynamite, frail, guard, inflate, kidnap, pillow, pinafore, program, scrap, scuff.

2. Algae.

3. Chicken.

4. Loess, because it is the only one that isn't an animal.

5. Toxic.

6. They are all chemical elements.

7. A type of amphibian; a soreness in the throat; a type of fastening on clothes; an arrangement of rails where one railroad track crosses another; a small, spiked holder used to keep flowers in place.

8. Yes, because a two-wheeled covered carriage could be pleasing in appearance.

True/False

9. False.

10. False.

11. False.

12. False.

13. False.

14. False.

15. True.

Word Chains

In a word chain, each word must begin with the last letter of the previous word. Each word must also fit the category of the word chain.

For example, suppose the category of a word chain is *fruits*. If the first word is *pear*, the next word must be a fruit that starts with the last letter, *r*, such as *rhubarb*.

Here is an example of a short word chain:

Fruits

pear

rhubarb

banana

apricot

tangerine

Directions

Now you try it. Continue the word chains started below. Make each chain as long as you possibly can, but add a minimum of five words to each.

Do not use any word more than once in a single chain.

Be sure to spell correctly. A misspelled word can ruin your entire chain.

Animals	**Foods**	**5-Letter Words**	**Makes of Cars**
deer	pizza	front	Chevrolet
rhinoceros	apple	train	Toyota
_____	_____	_____	_____
_____	_____	_____	_____
_____	_____	_____	_____
_____	_____	_____	_____
_____	_____	_____	_____

Answer Key
Word Chains

Answers will vary. Here are a few possibilities:

Animals	Foods	5-Letter Words	Makes of Cars
deer	pizza	front	Chevrolet
rhinoceros	apple	train	Toyota
snake	egg	nerve	Audi
elephant	granola	earth	Impala
tiger	asparagus	haven	Accord
rabbit	sugar	nasty	Dodge
tapir	rhubarb	youth	Explorer

Alphabet Story

See if you can write a story of exactly 26 sentences. But here is the hard part: Make the first sentence start with an *a*, the second with a *b*, the third with a *c* and so on through the alphabet. (For x you may cheat and use a word beginning with the prefix *ex.*)

Here's an example of how an alphabet story might start:

> **A** knock sounded at Joe's door one night. **B**ecause it was so late, he was rather nervous about answering it. **C**autiously, he went to the window and peeked out. **D**ebbie, his neighbor, stood there, holding an enormous package. **E**agerly, Joe went to the door. **F**linging it open, he saw then that Debbie had vanished. **G**erald Hayfield stood there instead. **H**e had an ominous grin on his face.

Now you try it. See if you can get through the entire alphabet with your story.

_____

_____

_____

_____

_____

_____

_____

_____

_____

_____

_____

_____

_____

_____

_____

_____

_____

Answer Key
Alphabet Story

Answers will vary. Here is one possibility:

Alex was not excited about the wedding. **B**ut he was happy that he would get to wear a tuxedo for the first time. **C**arolyn, his big sister, was engaged to marry Larry, a guy that Alex really liked. **D**ad and mom were also extremely happy about the announcement. **E**xcept, of course, for the fact that they had to pay for the wedding.

Friends that Carolyn had in college kept calling and asking if they could be in the wedding.

"**G**olly, but you are a popular bride," Alex told her.

"**H**ow can I possibly have eight bridesmaids?" Carolyn groaned.

"**I**f you have that many bridesmaids, your wedding will be way too big," Mom said.

"**J**anet and Irene fight all the time and Julie doesn't like Anna," Carolyn whined.

"**K**eep all this in mind as you decide what to do," warned Mom.

Larry, Carolyn's boyfriend, thought she was crazy to even consider all those women in one wedding.

"**M**y brother Mike and your brother Alex are the only guys I want in the wedding," Larry said. **N**icely, Carolyn told Larry he better think of some more guys to ask.

Over the next week, the "happy couple" argued everyday about the wedding.

"**P**erhaps they will never agree on this and break up," Alex's dad said with a smirk on his face.

Quietly, Alex worried about the situation and would listen outside the room where the couple argued. **R**ight after the arguing stopped, Alex would run into his bedroom. **S**lamming the door, he stamped his feet and pounded the bed.

"**T**hey better stop arguing, they better make up," he cried.

Unfortunately, the happy couple argued for two weeks straight. **V**ideos didn't help Alex feel any better like they usually did. **W**edding plans were put on hold. **Ex**citement stopped around the house until one morning when Alex was eating his Fruity Os.

"**Y**ou'll be happy to know Carolyn and Larry have agreed to have four men and four women in the wedding party and you'll be one of them," Alex's mom announced happily.

"**Z**ippadeedooda and Hurray," Alex yelled as he jumped up and down, relieved that Larry would still become his brother-in-law and that he would get to wear a tuxedo after all.

Name _____

Alliteration

You may not be aware of it, but we use something called *alliteration* quite often in our language, especially in ads, songs, commercials and poetry. Alliteration refers to the repetition of a consonant sound.

For example, this phrase illustrates alliteration: *a pair of penguins.*

So does this sentence: *Seven swans went swimming in Sweden.*

Here is a whole story that is alliterative:

A bunch of boys from the basketball club bounced balls into the busy bakery where Bob and Betty Beasley were baking brownies for the boxers Bruno Brigs and Boffo Benchley, who had a bout scheduled at the big boxing ring at Buckingham Stadium that day. Bruno and Boffo both loved brownies and always bought big batches before they boxed. They both believed brownies brought them luck.

But the boys from the basketball club were hungry as bears. They bought so many bags of brownies that there were none left for Bruno and Boffo. Bruno and Boffo had to box without them.

Because Bruno and Boffo believed their bodies needed brownies, they boxed badly. Their fans booed. Bruno and Boffo burst into tears.

The boys from the basketball club watched. They didn't boo. They just burped from eating too many brownies.

Now you try some alliteration:

1. Write a sentence describing a dog, using lots of *d* sounds. _____
   _____

2. Write a sentence about a car, using a lot of *c* sounds. _____
   _____

3. Write an alliterative story, using whatever letter you wish for the alliteration. See if you can make your story at least ten sentences long, using as much alliteration as possible.

   _____
   _____
   _____
   _____
   _____
   _____
   _____
   _____

Answer Key
Alliteration

Answers will vary. Here are some possibilities:

1. Dudley is a dark brown dingo who dances until dawn with dalmatians.

2. Cooper is constantly cleaning crickets out of his Chrysler.

3. Paolo the pig was just plain tired of his owner, Peggy Plantz, putting perfume on him. Every week Peggy paid Paul Pinkertone nine pennies for a bottle of Perfect Pansy Perfume. Paolo thought Perfect Pansy was rather putrid smelling. But he was a pleasant pig, eager to please, so he pretended he didn't mind. That didn't last long. He finally had to say something. "Pardon me, Peggy," he said one day, as she doused him with Perfect Pansy. "I much prefer Peppy Pickle perfume to this kind you always purchase for me. I find Perfect Pansy a little bit . . . oh, *pungent*."

   "Paolo!" Peggy cried. "I'm so pleased you professed your opinions." She popped out the door right then and purchased the proper perfume.

Similes

A simile is a comparison that uses the words *like* or *as*. For example, if you say, "I'm as hungry as a bear," you are using a simile. You are comparing your hunger to a bear's hunger.

We use similes in our speech and in our writing all the time. Why? Because they make our language more interesting and more descriptive.

However, we also have a tendency to use common similes over and over again until they aren't interesting and descriptive anymore. They become dull from overuse. For example, the first time someone said "quiet as a mouse," that phrase was probably very effective. But now it has been used so much that no one hearing it ever stops to consider how quiet a mouse really is.

Directions

Complete each of the following similes in a new, fresh way. Don't use the phrase that probably comes to your mind first. For example, in completing the phrase "quiet as a _____," don't say *mouse*. Instead try something new, like "quiet as a spider tiptoeing across its web."

1. Gentle as a _____

   _____

2. Hungry as a _____

   _____

3. Skinny as a _____

   _____

4. Fat as a _____

   _____

5. Ugly as a _____

   _____

6. Mad as a _____

   _____

7. Happy as a _____

   _____

8. Pretty as a _____

   _____

Answer Key
Similes

Answers will vary. Here are some possibilities:

1. Gentle as a dandelion seed floating across the crab grass.
2. Hungry as a soccer team after a six-hour tournament game.
3. Skinny as a popsicle stick, sideways.
4. Fat as a pregnant marshmallow.
5. Ugly as a hunk of cheddar cheese melting in the sun.
6. Mad as a mother whose children forgot to tell her about the parent-teacher conference today.
7. Happy as a football fan doing the wave.
8. Pretty as a maple tree turning colors in the October sun.

Name _____

Directions

For each category listed along the left side of the page, think of an appropriate word that begins with the letter at the top of the column. The first item is done for you.

	H	E	A	R	T	S
Fruits	huckleberry					
Kinds of Cars						
Names of Cartoon Characters						
Foreign Countries						
Things Many People Are Afraid Of						
Six-Letter Words						
Desserts						
Musical Instruments						

Answer Key
Hearts

Answers will vary. Here are some possibilities:

	H	E	A	R	T	S
Fruits	huckleberry	elderberry	apricot	raspberry	tangerine	strawberry
Kinds of Cars	Honda	Explorer	Accord	Riviera	Toyota	Saturn
Names of Cartoon Characters	Homer Simpson	Eeyore	Alley Oop	Roadrunner	Tasmanian Devil	Stimpy
Foreign Countries	Hungary	Ethiopia	Austria	Romania	Turkey	Saudi Arabia
Things Many People Are Afraid Of	haunted houses	extra-terrestrial beings	airplane flights	robbers	tarantulas	spiders
Six-Letter Words	heifer	entice	always	rabbit	tundra	school
Desserts	Hostess Twinkies	eclair	apple turnover	raisin pie	truffles	sundaes
Musical Instruments	harp	electric guitar	accordion	recorder	trumpet	string bass

Newspaper Scavenger Hunt

This game works well right before a vacation, after a newspaper unit or any time the students (and you!) need a break. It gives the students practice in skim reading, following directions and working together as a team. It also helps them become familiar with the various features of a newspaper.

Materials

- At least two copies of a daily newspaper for each team. (They can all be different issues.)
- One "Newspaper Scavenger Hunt List" for each team (page 25).
- Tokens. (Dried beans, chips, buttons or play money work well.)
- Scissors for each team.

Organization

A number of items on the "Newspaper Scavenger Hunt List" have blanks that need to be typed or filled in with current information before photocopying. Complete these items, as follows:

6. the names of two current movies
13. the name of a city currently in the news
18. the name of a current rock star
25. an issue currently making news
29. a current world leader
34. the name of a sports star
38. the name of a football, baseball or basketball team

Have the students sit together in teams of four, as far as possible from other groups. Pass out newspapers, scissors and the "Newspaper Scavenger Hunt List" to each team.

Instructions

Read the instructions on the "Newspaper Scavenger Hunt List" aloud, as the students follow along. Answer any questions, and then have the students begin.

(Note: When a *runner* brings up an item(s) to be checked, be sure to check off the item on the team's official answer sheet so that it can't be used again by that team. Take the item and give the team one token.)

At the end of the game, the team with the most tokens wins. Even better, announce ahead of time that *every* team that earns a designated number of tokens is a winner.

Suggestions

- It usually works best to play the game for two or three class periods. It is helpful to give each team an additional newspaper on the second or third day of the game, so that the students have fresh material to work with.

- Newspapers for each group need not be identical. In fact, it is better for each team to have different, though complete, newspapers.

- Be picky. Insist that each item be exactly as described on the *Newspaper Scavenger Hunt List* — or the team receives no token. This encourages careful reading.

- After the students understand the game and have received a few tokens, announce that, in the future, runners will need to bring a minimum of three items at a time for checking. Otherwise, checking can get a bit hectic.

- You may want to give each group more than one *Newspaper Scavenger Hunt List*. If so, be sure the students designate only one of the handouts as their official answer sheet. The runner should bring only that sheet to the teacher with items to be checked.

- Every day at the end of the period, have each team turn in a neat bundle of newspapers, with the team's *Newspaper Scavenger Hunt List* on top. Collect the tokens for that day and record the amount so that you can give the team back the same number of tokens the next day.

Names of team members: _____

_____

_____

_____

The purpose of the Newspaper Scavenger Hunt is to find as many as possible of the items on the Newspaper Scavenger Hunt List, below. Your team will receive a token for each item found. The team with the most tokens at the end of the game will be the winner.

Instructions

- Write the names of your team members at the top of this sheet. This will be your official answer sheet.

- Choose one person to be your team's *runner*. Only the runner may take newspaper items to your teacher to be checked.

- When you find an item, cut it out and write its "*Newspaper Scavenger Hunt List*" number on it. Then your team's runner should bring the item, with the official answer sheet, to your teacher to be checked. You will receive one token for each correct item. (Note: It is possible that your newspapers may not contain one or two of the "*Newspaper Scavenger Hunt List*" items required. That's okay. Remember that a scavenger hunt involves skill, cooperation and luck. Do the best you can with what you have.)

Newspaper Scavenger Hunt List

1. an account of a school board meeting
2. a cartoon that shows an animal other than a cat, a dog or a penguin
3. an editorial
4. an obituary for someone over 75
5. an ad for a job paying over $20,000 per year
6. an ad for _____ or _____
7. an article about an animal
8. an ad for a discount air fare
9. an article mentioning a religious leader
10. the name of the editor of the newspaper
11. an account of a burglary or robbery
12. a letter to the editor against something (Be able to say what.)
13. an article about someone or something in _____
14. a weather forecast
15. a horoscope prediction for an Aquarius

16. an article about a child

17. a quotation by a coach

18. an article mentioning _____

19. an article about anyone whose last name begins with a T

20. an article about anything happening in a European country

21. the score of a game where the losing team lost by over 18 points

22. an account of a wedding where the husband's last name begins with an M

23. a quotation by the president of the United States

24. a positive review of a movie

25. an article about _____

26. a letter to an advice columnist about a problem concerning a son or daughter

27. an article about a person with the same first or last name as someone on your team

28. an article mentioning the governor of your state

29. an article mentioning _____

30. an ad for a free kitten

31. an article about a fashion or a clothing fad

32. an article about a natural disaster (flood, hurricane, tornado, etc.)

33. an article mentioning anyone with five vowels in his/her name

34. an article mentioning _____

35. a recipe for something containing sugar

36. a picture of a foreign leader

37. an article about a woman

38. an article mentioning _____

39. an ad for a five-bedroom house

40. an article about a television show or a television star

41. an ad for a Mexican-food restaurant

42. an article mentioning any kind of reptile

43. a book review

44. a crossword puzzle

45. an article mentioning your state capital

46. an article about the results of a trial

47. an article about a medical discovery

48. an ad for a garage sale

49. an ad with the business owner's picture in it

50. a "cents-off" coupon for a food product

Name _____

 Animals

There are 50 animals hidden below. Unscramble the letters in each item so that you spell the animal's name. The first one is done for you.

1. goonarak   _____kangaroo_____

2. osmoe _____

3. oserinchor _____

4. dapna _____

5. largloi _____

6. eshep _____

7. dramalanse _____

8. fragfie _____

9. braze _____

10. phalteen _____

11. nillachich _____

12. ruppocine _____

13. naguai _____

14. dropale _____

15. swarlu _____

16. ubrocai _____

17. dree _____

18. nukks _____

19. pinkmuch _____

20. yoctoe _____

21. clame _____

22. acronoc _____

23. osume _____

24. planotee _____

25. eltrut _____

26. shero _____

27. tabcob _____

28. neomelach _____

29. mussopo _____

30. regit _____

31. drazil _____

32. glataroil _____

33. dricoloce _____

34. fretre _____

35. estoroit _____

36. whockudoc _____

37. treeatan _____

38. trote _____

39. lirquers _____

40. evebra _____

41. kravadar _____

42. kay _____

43. gip _____

44. rabe _____

45. grof _____

46. chorits _____

47. otag _____

48. act _____

49. olni _____

50. ofalbuf _____

Answer Key
Animals

1. kangaroo
2. moose
3. rhinoceros
4. panda
5. gorilla
6. sheep
7. salamander
8. giraffe
9. zebra
10. elephant
11. chinchilla
12. porcupine
13. iguana
14. leopard
15. walrus
16. caribou
17. deer
18. skunk
19. chipmunk
20. coyote
21. camel
22. raccoon
23. mouse
24. antelope
25. turtle
26. horse
27. bobcat
28. chameleon
29. opossum
30. tiger
31. lizard
32. alligator
33. crocodile
34. ferret
35. tortoise
36. woodchuck
37. anteater
38. otter
39. squirrel
40. beaver
41. aardvark
42. yak
43. pig
44. bear
45. frog
46. ostrich
47. goat
48. cat
49. lion
50. buffalo

Name _____

Directions

For each category listed along the left side of the page, think of an appropriate word that begins with the letter at the top of the column. The first item is done for you.

	S	P	R	I	N	G
Colors	scarlet					
Names of Restaurants						
Adjectives Used to Describe a Person						
Items of Clothing						
Things You Might Put on a Pizza						
Animals						
Boys' Names						
Words That End in the Letter E						

Answer Key
Spring

Answers will vary. Here are some possibilities:

	S	P	R	I	N	G
Colors	scarlet	purple	red	indigo	navy blue	gray
Names of Restaurants	Subway	Pizza Hut	Red Lobster	International House of Pancakes	New China	Godfather's Pizza
Adjectives Used to Describe a Person	sophisticated	pretty	roly-poly	interesting	nice	gorgeous
Items of Clothing	shirt	pants	robe	itchy underwear	nylons	gown
Things You Might Put on a Pizza	sardines	pineapple	red pepper	Italian sausage	nonfat cheese	ground beef
Animals	salamander	porcupine	rabbit	iguana	newt	giraffe
Boys' Names	Stephen	Paul	Robert	Isaac	Nathan	George
Words That End in *E*	software	plane	release	insane	name	graduate

Categories

This game is active and can be noisy, but it keeps the students interested and their minds alert. Once you have the cards made, you can keep the game handy for whenever you have an extra ten minutes at the end of class.

Materials

Make a set of alphabet cards, each card showing one letter of the alphabet. Make the cards large enough for students to see easily. You may want to leave out difficult letters like *x* and make two or three each of some other letters, like *m* or *s*.

Organization

Divide the class into two teams. The students can remain at their desks to play, or you can sit on a stool and have them gather around, sitting on the floor on either side of you. Choose a scorekeeper.

Instructions

Tell the students that you will announce a category. Then, when you hold up an alphabet card, they are to try to think of something that begins with that letter and that fits the announced category. The first person to call out an answer wins a point for his or her team. After a word wins a point for a team, the word can't be used again if the same letter reappears.

Categories can be simple or difficult, silly or serious. Here are just a few suggestions:

- kinds of candy
- characters in *To Kill a Mockingbird*
- verbs
- NFL football teams
- nice words to describe your teacher
- animals
- brand names of beauty products
- things that are sweet
- cartoon characters
- boys' names
- girls' names
- cities
- games you play with a ball

Suggestions

- To keep the noise level down, you may want to have the students whisper rather than shout out answers.

- Keep the game moving fast, changing categories frequently. If no one comes up with an answer right away, move on. Make sure the scorekeeper is someone who can keep up, putting marks on the board quickly as you indicate which side gets a point each time you hold up an alphabet card.

- Don't let the game degenerate into arguments about points. Explain that often several students may give a correct answer at nearly the same time. You will choose who you think came first and give that person's team the point. Admit that you may sometimes make a mistake in one team's favor but that you are likely, the next time, to make a mistake in the other team's favor. Any mistakes are bound to even out in the long run and aren't worth fussing over, especially when points are earned as quickly as they are in this game. If students call out answers at exactly the same time, call it a tie and go on to the next alphabet card.

- Keep the game light. This is a game where the points usually become unimportant as the students get involved in coming up with answers quickly.

Name _____

Getting Acquainted

Find someone else in class:

1. Who was born the same month as you _____

2. Who wears the same size shoe as you _____

3. Who was born in the same state as you _____

4. Who has the same number of brothers as you _____

5. Whose mother's first name is the same as your mother's _____

6. Who has lived in another state _____

7. Who has visited Disney World _____

8. Who likes anchovies _____

9. Whose father's first name is *Jim* _____

10. Who has more than two cats _____

11. Who has a Saint Bernard _____

12. Who has the same first or last name as you _____

13. Who has traveled to a foreign country _____

14. Whose favorite subject is science _____

15. Who moved to your city or town in the last three months _____

16. Who likes Brussels sprouts _____

17. Who has a hamster _____

18. Who takes piano lessons _____

19. Who is wearing the same color blouse, shirt or top as you _____

20. Who has an older brother or sister who attends your school _____

21. Whose last name has the same number of letters as yours _____

22. Who is wearing a non-digital watch _____

23. Who competes in swimming or gymnastics _____

24. Who has a horse _____

25. Who knows how to tie flies _____

26. Whose middle name is *Ann* _____

27. Whose ear is pierced more than once _____

28. Who is using a *Bic* pen _____

29. Who has physical education second period _____

30. Who has seven letters in his or her first name _____

Directions

For each category listed along the left side of the page, think of an appropriate word that begins with the letter at the top of the column. The first item is done for you.

Name _____

	G	O	B	L	I	N
Things You Might Put on a Sub Sandwich	guacamole					
Major League Baseball Teams						
Items You Might Receive in Your Trick or-Treat Bag						
Synonyms for *Horrible*						
Famous People from History (last names)						
Brand Names of Clothing						
Proper Nouns of Six or More Letters						
Words that Rhyme with *Scare*						

Answer Key
Goblin

Answers will vary. Here are some possibilities:

	G	O	B	L	I	N
Things You Might Put on a Sub Sandwich	guacamole	onions	bacon	lettuce	Italian dressing	non-fat cheese
Major League Baseball Teams	Giants	Orioles	Boston Red Sox	Los Angeles Dodgers	Indians	New York Yankees
Items You Might Receive in Your Trick-or-Treat Bag	gum	oranges	Baby Ruth	licorice	individually-wrapped Snickers	Nestle Crunch
Synonyms for *Horrible*	ghastly	obnoxious	bad	lewd	ignominious	nasty
Famous People from History (last names)	Indira Gandhi	J. Robert Oppenheimer	Elizabeth Blackwell	Meriwether Lewis	Washington Irving	Richard Nixon
Brand Names of Clothing	Gap	OshKosh	Bugle Boy	Levi	Izod	Nike
Proper Nouns of Six or More Letters	Gertrude	Oregon	Bradley	London	Iceland	Nebraska
Words that Rhyme with *Scare*	glare	outerwear	bear	lair	impair	nightmare

Antonyms

Antonyms are words that are opposite in meaning, like *tall / short* or *laugh / cry*.

Listed below are pairs of antonyms. However, all the vowels are missing. See if you can separate each pair of antonyms and replace the missing vowels.

Example:

bgsmll _____big/small_____

1. fstslw _____
2. htcld _____
3. nncntglty _____
4. smthrgh _____
5. hppysd _____
6. wrmcld _____
7. gvtk _____
8. lftrght _____
9. pdwn _____
10. lghtdrk _____
11. wtdry _____
12. gdbd _____
13. nt _____

14. srswt _____
15. ftthn _____
16. ndrvr _____
17. ststnd _____
18. ldyng _____
19. crkdstrght _____
20. smlfrwn _____
21. tpbttm _____
22. glybtfl _____
23. wrngrght _____
24. blckwht _____
25. lvht _____

Make Your Own Puzzle

Now think of at least five more antonyms. Then make your own antonym puzzle by leaving out the vowels and moving the remaining letters together. When you are finished, share your antonym puzzle with someone else.

Answer Key
Antonyms

1. fast/slow
2. hot/cold
3. innocent/guilty
4. smooth/rough
5. happy/sad
6. warm/cold
7. give/take
8. left/right
9. up/down
10. light/dark
11. wet/dry
12. good/bad
13. in/out
14. sour/sweet
15. fat/thin
16. under/over
17. sit/stand
18. old/young
19. crooked/straight
20. smile/frown
21. top/bottom
22. ugly/beautiful
23. wrong/right
24. black/white
25. love/hate

Make Your Own Puzzle

Answers will vary.

Build a Sentence #1

For each list of words below, see if you can make up one sentence that uses all the words on the list. To do this, you may add words before or after the words on the list, but you may not change the order. The final sentence must make sense, though it may be a bit farfetched! The first one has been done for you.

Word Lists	Sentences
shattering **car** **struggle** **if** **cost** **children**	We heard a **shattering** noise when the **car** drove over the wall and people began to **struggle** as **if** they were afraid the accident might **cost** the **children** their lives.
scream **wicked** **home** **not** **play** **imagination**	
song **mansion** **equal** **hot** **after** **two** **royal**	
agree **or** **chip** **him** **city** **ordered** **confidence** **telephone**	

Answer Key
Build a Sentence #1

Answers will vary. Some possibilities:

Word Lists	Sentences
shattering car struggle if cost children	We heard a **shattering** noise when the **car** drove over the wall and people began to **struggle** as if they were afraid the accident might **cost** the **children** their lives.
scream wicked home not play imagination	I remember the loud **scream** that came from the **wicked** owl sitting on the roof of the **home** where it was **not** a good place to **play**, even if you used your **imagination**.
song mansion equal hot after two royal	I heard a **song** about a magic **mansion** where everyone is **equal** and on **hot** nights **after** midnight **two** servants give everyone the **royal** treatment by fanning them with huge palm fronds.
agree or chip him city ordered confidence telephone	Whether you **agree or** not, that **chip** of diamond given by **him** to that **city** girl was **ordered** with **confidence** over the **telephone** without even a credit card.

Build a Sentence #2

For each list of words below, see if you can make up one sentence that uses all the words on the list. To do this, you may add words before or after the words on the list, but you may not change the order. The final sentence must make sense, although it may be a bit far-fetched! The first one has been done for you.

Word Lists	Sentences
picnic enormous toddler gasp hope hungry	At the church **picnic**, an **enormous** Saint Bernard accidentally knocked over a **toddler**, who let out a **gasp** and said, "I sure **hope** that dog isn't **hungry**!"
fingernails trees when fill for homework	
silly because accordion cold before six cruel	
laughed teeth fighting to still not grow elephant	

Answer Key
Build a Sentence #2

Answers will vary. Some possibilities:

Word Lists	Sentences
picnic enormous toddler gasp hope hungry	At the church **picnic**, an **enormous** Saint Bernard accidentally knocked over a **toddler**, who let out a gasp and said, "I sure **hope** that dog isn't **hungry!**"
fingernails trees when fill for homework	I was filing my **fingernails** under the aspen **trees** when he asked me to **fill** the glass **for** Jane so she could do her **homework**.
silly because accordion cold before six cruel	Dr. Runzel is so **silly because** she plays the **accordion** to treat all her patients with influenza or the common **cold before** they contract the **six**-day jeebies, a **cruel** illness.
laughed teeth fighting to still not grow elephant	After Gordon **laughed** so hard he hit his **teeth** on the floor, he was **fighting to** sit **still** and **not** cry, for he knew his tears would **grow** into **elephant**-sized sobs.

Name _____

Tongue Twisters

At some time or another, all of us have stumbled over tongue twisters — those tricky combinations of words that are very difficult to say. For example, try saying this short tongue twister three times in a row:

Mixed biscuits

Difficult, isn't it? Here are three more well-known tongue twisters:

- *Rubber baby buggy bumpers*
- *She sells sea shells down by the seashore.*
- *Peter Piper picked a peck of pickled peppers.*

What makes tongue twisters so difficult to say? Here are a few characteristics:

- Frequent repetition of a consonant sound. Example: the *p* in "**P**eter **P**iper **p**icked a **p**eck of **p**ickled **pepp**ers."

- Use of words that are almost — but not quite — the same. Example: *she* and *sea*, *sells* and *shells*.

- Use of sounds that are similar, especially when one occurs right after the other. Example: the *ix* and *is* sounds in "m*ix*ed b*is*cuits."

Try writing some tongue twisters of your own. See how difficult you can make them, testing them by saying them out loud.

1. Write a tongue twister that uses the *c* and *cr* sounds frequently.

   _____

   _____

2. Write a tongue twister that uses the words *best* and *bets*.

   _____

   _____

3. Write a tongue twister that uses the words *sisters* and *slipped*.

   _____

   _____

Answer Key
Tongue Twisters

Answers will vary. Here are some possibilities:

1. Chris's constant cries create craziness and crisis.
2. Beth's bets are best before breakfast.
3. Six sick sisters slipped on slick sidewalks.

Name _____

Letter Pairs

Add more letters to each pair of letters below to make a word. You may not add letters between the pair of letters — only before or after.

For example, if the letter pair is *dg*, you could form the word *edge*. You could not form the word *dog* because you would have to insert a letter between *d* and *g*.

The object of the game is to make the lowest score possible, so try to add as few letters as you can. Your score for each pair is the total number of letters you have added to make a word. For example, your score for the word *edge* would be two points because you added two letters.

You will be penalized ten points for any pair you are unable to complete. Good luck!

	Word	**Score**			**Word**	**Score**
1. od	_____	_____	11. tl	_____	_____
2. tp	_____	_____	12. lp	_____	_____
3. pb	_____	_____	13. os	_____	_____
4. re	_____	_____	14. dw	_____	_____
5. ts	_____	_____	15. ip	_____	_____
6. nc	_____	_____	16. gd	_____	_____
7. ld	_____	_____	17. wb	_____	_____
8. ei	_____	_____	18. at	_____	_____
9. ra	_____	_____	19. ch	_____	_____
10. wh	_____	_____	20. ro	_____	_____

TOTAL #1 _____   TOTAL #2 _____

Total #1 _____

Total #2 _____

10 x ____ (number of pairs not completed) ____

FINAL SCORE _____

Answer Key
Letter Pairs

Answers will vary. Here are some possibilities:

Word Score

#	Pair	Word	Score
1.	od	odd	1
2.	tp	potpie	4
3.	pb	cupboard	6
4.	re	ore	1
5.	ts	its	1
6.	nc	once	2
7.	ld	old	1
8.	ei	rein	2
9.	ra	era	1
10.	wh	who	1

TOTAL #1 __20__

Word Score

#	Pair	Word	Score
11.	tl	title	2
12.	lp	help	2
13.	os	toss	2
14.	dw	dwarf	3
15.	ip	tip	1
16.	gd	kingdom	5
17.	wb	cowboy	4
18.	at	cat	1
19.	ch	itch	2
20.	ro	row	1

TOTAL #2 __24__

Total #1 __20__

Total #2 __24__

10 x __0__ (number of pairs not completed) __0__

FINAL SCORE __44__

Name _____

 # The Race Is On!

How fast can your group work as a team? See how many points you can score in the time allowed by completing as many as possible of the items below.

You may do the items in any order. Keep track of your own score at the side as you go. The number of points possible for each item is indicated after it.

Put all your answers on a separate sheet(s) of paper.

1. List the names of 10 popular singers, in alphabetical order by their last names. (10 points)

2. Write down the complete last name of the tallest member of your group. Using the letters of that name, make as many new words as possible. If a letter appears only once in the name, it can be used only once in any word. (2 points per new word)

3. List, in alphabetical order, ten places where you might buy a hamburger in your city or town. (10 points)

4. List 10 words that begin and end with the same letter. Example: *Bomb*. (10 points)

5. List 15 words with double letters. Example: *Butter*. (15 points)

6. Write the words to any nursery rhyme. (5 points)

7. List 10 pairs of people in your school who have the same first or last names. Be sure to list both names. Example: *Jennifer Adams* and *Jennifer Delaney*. (10 points)

8. Make a list of 25 items that fit a certain category. You may make up to five lists. Use the following categories for your lists: *Countries of the World, Makes of Cars, Television Shows, Candy Bars, Song Titles*. (10 points per list)

9. List 10 words with only one vowel. The words must be at least four letters long. (10 points)

10. List 15 words that rhyme with *hat*. (15 points)

Answer Key
The Race Is On!

Answers will vary. Here are some possibilities:

#1
1. Eminem
2. Faith Hill
3. Alan Jackson
4. Kid Rock
5. Jennifer Lopez
6. Dave Matthews
7. Tim McGraw
8. Nelly
9. Britney Spears
10. Shania Twain

#2
Hosek: she, hose, shoe, he, hoe

#3
1. Applebee's
2. Bennigan's
3. Burger King
4. Chili's
5. McDonald's
6. Red Robin
7. Hardee's
8. SportsCaster
9. Sonic Drive-In
10. Wendy's

#4
1. dad
2. mom
3. level
4. smiles
5. roar
6. tenant
7. kick
8. dead
9. moratorium
10. gag

#5
1. express
2. impress
3. book
4. school
5. dessert
6. commit
7. happy
8. off

9. bottom
10. loose
11. marriage
12. jolly
13. reed
14. effort
15. willow

#6
Jack and Jill went up the hill to fetch a pail of water; Jack fell down and broke his crown, and Jill came tumbling after.

#7
John Barnes/ John Montoya
Chad Sullivan/ Lindsey Sullivan
Tiffany Jamison/ Tiffany Roy

#8
Countries of the World
1. Argentina
2. Brazil
3. United States
4. Mexico
5. Canada
6. Costa Rica
7. Guatemala
8. South Africa
9. Kenya
10. Egypt
11. Israel
12. China
13. Japan
14. Iran
15. Iraq
16. Saudi Arabia
17. France
18. Italy
19. Spain
20. Poland
21. Hungary
22. England
23. Luxembourg
24. Germany
25. Iceland

Makes of Cars
1. Honda
2. Ford
3. Toyota
4. Mercedes-Benz
5. BMW
6. Volvo
7. KIA
8. Subaru
9. Saturn
10. Chevrolet
11. Nissan
12. Hyundai
13. Isuzu
14. Volkswagen
15. Jeep
16. Audi
17. Buick
18. Porsche
19. Mazda
20. Dodge
21. Saab
22. Cadillac
23. Lincoln
24. Jaguar
25. Geo

Television Shows
1. Gilmore Girls
2. Seinfeld
3. Simpsons
4. Dawson's Creek
5. Fear Factor
6. Survivor
7. The Bachelor
8. Everybody Loves Raymond
9. Jerry Springer
10. Friends
11. Dateline
12. Ally McBeal
13. 60 Minutes
14. 20/20
15. E.R.
16. Cosby Show
17. CSI
18. Saturday Night Live
19. Weakest Link
20. Jeopardy!
21. Wheel of Fortune

22. COPS
23. American Idol
24. Sesame Street
25. That 70's Show

Candy Bars
1. Heath
2. KitKat
3. Skor
4. Mounds
5. Almond Joy
6. Snickers
7. Milky Way
8. Caramello
9. Tootsie Roll
10. Hershey's Bar
11. Dove
12. Twix
13. 3 Musketeers
14. Mars
15. Nestle Crunch
16. 5th Avenue
17. Butterfinger
18. Big Hunk
19. O'Henry!
20. 100 Grand
21. Baby Ruth
22. PayDay
23. Mr. Goodbar
24. Whatchamacallit
25. Symphony

Song Titles
1. Amazing Grace
2. Mr. Bojangles
3. Superstition
4. Roxanne
5. Copacabana
6. Unforgettable
7. Golden Slippers
8. Africa
9. Rock-a-Bye Baby
10. Crazy
11. Thriller
12. Crash
13. Strange Fruit
14. Jingle Bells
15. O Holy Night
16. Silent Night
17. Tennessee Waltz

18. Love Potion #9
19. Heartbreak Hotel
20. America
21. Jailhouse Rock
22. La Bamba
23. One
24. Allentown
25. Piano Man

#9
1. trash
2. troll
3. press
4. print
5. gray
6. black
7. tips
8. word
9. march
10. high

#10
1. cat
2. fat
3. that
4. sat
5. mat
6. bat
7. gnat
8. pat
9. vat
10. scat
11. chat
12. brat
13. at
14. spat
15. rat

Shamrocks

There are many words hidden in the word *shamrock*. See if you can find a word that fits each definition below. Remember, you can use only the letters in *shamrock* for your answers.

1. Something to eat with eggs _____

2. Something hard _____

3. To wander here and there _____

4. A knitted item you wear on one foot _____

5. Something to drive _____

6. To squash _____

7. What you have when you break out in red marks _____

8. Money in your pocket _____

9. What injured people often go into _____

10. A run-down building _____

11. To study at the last minute for a test _____

12. An upper limb _____

13. To hurt _____

14. Two cars running into one another _____

15. A toothed animal of the sea _____

Now see if you can find five more words hidden in *shamrock*. Write definitions for them below.

16. _____

17. _____

18. _____

19. _____

20. _____

Answer Key
Shamrocks

1. ham
2. rock
3. roam
4. sock
5. car
6. mash
7. rash
8. cash
9. shock
10. shack
11. cram
12. arm
13. harm
14. crash
15. shark
16.–20. Answers will vary. Possibilities: ram, sack, cork, mark, smash

Life and Death

This game is effective when the class has been talking about symbolism — or whenever you want to stimulate creativity. If the students have a bit of trouble at first, don't give up. Given a bit more time, they usually come up with some very clever material.

Instructions

Tell the students that there is a disagreement among a group of scholars. Some of them say that your classroom was designed by an architect to symbolize death. Others say it was designed to symbolize life.

Have the students look around and think about the issue. Is the room windowless? Perhaps that's because the architect wanted the room to resemble a coffin. Are there lights overhead? Perhaps the architect meant them to represent one of the earth's basic life-giving sources, the sun.

Divide the class in half. Tell the students on one side that they are to help prove that the room symbolizes life. Tell the students on the other side that they are to help prove that the room symbolizes death. Have all the students brainstorm silently for five minutes, writing down anything they can think of that might help prove their side of the argument.

After five minutes, have the students on each side meet in small groups to share their ideas and to come up with others. Each group should pick a spokesperson to address the class and present the group's best arguments.

Suggestions

- Encourage the students to have some fun with this, and emphasize that there are no wrong or right answers. If groups seem to be having trouble, give them a few ideas to get them started.

- Encourage the spokespersons to put some life into their presentations, hamming it up, if they like. In fact, you may want to let the spokespersons prepare their presentations for the next class period, to give them more time.

Directions

For each category listed along the left side of the page, think of an appropriate word that begins with the letter at the top of the column. The first item is done for you.

	T	I	N	S	E	L
Girls' Names	Teresa					
Vegetables						
Things You Might Find During Winter						
U.S. Cities						
Last Names of Famous Athletes						
One-Syllable Words						
Colors						
Verbs (action words)						

Answer Key
Tinsel

Answers will vary. Here are some possibilities:

	T	I	N	S	E	L
Girls' Names	Teresa	Isabelle	Nancy	Sylvia	Emma	Luanne
Vegetables	turnip	iceberg lettuce	new potatoes	string beans	endive	leeks
Things You Might Find During Winter	turtlenecks	ice hockey	New Year's Eve parties	snow	egg nog	low temperatures
U.S. Cities	Tucson	Indianapolis	New Haven	Sante Fe	Elgin	Lincoln
Last Names of Famous Athletes	Vinny Testaverde	Raghib Isamail	Joe Namath	Picabo Street	John Elway	Lisa Leslie
One-Syllable Words	tough	inn	night	sun	eat	leg
Colors	turquoise	ivory	navy	scarlet	eggshell	lavender
Verbs (action words)	tumble	injure	nodded	swim	escape	lunge

Dear Edna

This game is good for one of those leftover Fridays when you don't want to begin a new unit. It can also be used at the end of a unit on letter writing.

Instructions

Tell the students there is a new advice columnist, Edna. They have a once-in-a-lifetime opportunity to get a personal, immediate reply from Edna. All they need to do is write to Edna about a problem, any problem at all that is appropriate for sharing in class. Problems can be serious, humorous, real or imaginary.

Give the class 10 or 15 minutes to write their letters to Edna. If they have time, they may even write more than one letter, using a different piece of paper for each letter. Insist that the students sign the letters with a fictional name.

Collect the letters. Then pass them back so that each student receives a letter other than the one he or she wrote. Each student then acts as Edna, writing the answer to the problem presented in the letter he or she has received. Students should answer on the same page as the letter.

Students who finish quickly can answer another letter. Or you may want to let more than one person answer each letter, with the first person designated as Edna #1 and the second as her twin sister, Edna #2.

Have the students pass in the letters and answers. Read as many letters and answers as time allows. Then post the remaining letters on a bulletin board so that all the students can read their letters and answers the next day.

Suggestions

- It is a good idea, of course, to scan a letter and its answer before reading it aloud or posting it. In fact, you may want to postpone sharing the letters until the next day.

- Often, this game is more fun the second time around. Students know what is going on then and will usually write more interesting letters.

Holiday Challenge

This game is great for the week before Christmas vacation. It is challenging and keeps students interested for two or three class periods.

Materials

- Copies of the "Holiday Challenge List" for each group. (Before photocopying these, fill in names for the blanks in items #15, #38, and #60. Use the names of other teachers, the principal or someone else well-known to the students.)

- An official answer sheet for each group. (This can be a piece of notebook paper numbered from one to sixty, with group members' names at the top. Some answers will require more than one line, so each group should have extra paper to attach to the official answer sheet when necessary.)

- Ordinary classroom reference materials like grammar books, literature books and dictionaries. (It is a good idea to bring in some extra materials, as well, like a set of encyclopedias, an almanac and an atlas.)

- Tokens. (Dried beans, play money, chips or buttons work well. You will need a fairly large quantity of whatever you select.)

Organization

Divide the class into groups of four. Students should sit together, as far as possible from other groups.

Read aloud the first paragraph from the "Holiday Challenge List." Then tell the students that they are on their own. They should read the directions carefully and begin.

Suggestions

- Emphasize that the "Holiday Challenge" is an exercise in following instructions. If students seem confused at first, keep referring them to the instructions. They will quickly catch on and realize that *they* must figure out what to do.

- Allow teams to have a negative balance of tokens. At first students will almost certainly guess at some answers, but when they go "in the hole," they will learn to be more careful.

- Have fun with the game. The classroom will probably be noisy, but it will be a productive kind of noise.

Name _____

This is an exercise in following directions, cooperating and using your ingenuity. The purpose is to earn tokens by completing as many as possible of the numbered items on the "Holiday Challenge List," below. The group with the most tokens at the end of the game will be the winner.

Instructions

- Write your group members' names at the top of your official answer sheet.

- Choose one member of your group to act as "runner." When you have completed one or more items on the "Holiday Challenge List," the runner should bring your official answer sheet to the teacher to be checked.

- Only the designated runner in each group may turn in answers. All written answers must be on your official answer sheet.

- To complete the items on "Holiday Challenge List," you may use any resources in this room — except for another group's answer sheet.

- You may complete the items in any order.

- Correctly completed items will be awarded the number of tokens specified in parentheses after each item. Incorrect answers will cause your group to lose double the specified number of tokens for that item.

- Each answer that is written must be legible and spelled correctly. Otherwise it will be considered incorrect. BE CAREFUL!

Holiday Challenge List

- You must turn in all challenge lists, answer sheets and tokens at the end of each period that the game is played. You may not copy questions to complete outside of class, although you are free to try to find the answers to any items you can *remember*.

1. What is a *wallaby*? (1)

2. Write down three words that are exactly the same, spelled frontwards or backwards. (1)

3. Who wrote "The Secret Life of Walter Mitty"? (1)

4. If you were born July 25, what is your zodiac sign? (1)

5. Name Santa's eight reindeer. (3)

6. Who won the Super Bowl in 1979? (2)

7. Use to, *two* and *too* correctly in one sentence. (1)

8. What is the square root of 169? (2)

9. In what city does *Romeo and Juliet* take place? (2)

10. Mount Vernon is on the _____ River. (1)

11. What are "city sidewalks, busy sidewalks" dressed in? (2)

12. Name 10 spices. (2)

13. Write down 25 words that end in *r*. (3)

14. Draw a picture of a *volute*. (1)

15. What is _____ 's cat's name? (4)

16. Are there three people in this room wearing non-digital watches? If so, who are they?

17. Write a message in which each word starts with a successive letter in the words HAPPY HOLIDAYS. The first word should begin with *H*, the second with *A*, the third with *P* and so forth. The message must make sense and may include more than one sentence. (5)

18. Name five books of the Old Testament. (2)

19. List the eight parts of speech. (2)

20. How many days long is Hanukkah? (2)

21. Write down five uses for a broken Christmas tree ornament. (2)

22. Write a holiday poem called "Joy." It must be at least eight lines long. At least four lines must rhyme. (5)

23. Who defeated George Foreman in the heavyweight boxing championship bout of 1974? (2)

24. Give the comparative and superlative forms of the word *good*. (2)

25. What is the total number of *e*'s in the last names of the members of your group? (1)

26. In what country is the Dnieper River? (2)

27. Write a sentence with a participle phrase. Underline the phrase. (2)

28. Who is the present U.S. Secretary of State? (1)

29. Write down six adjectives that could be used to describe a car. (2)

30. "In the meadow we shall build _____. And pretend that he is _____."(2)

31. Write down the titles of five of Shakespeare's plays. (2)

32. Ten centimeters equals _____ inches. (1)

33. What are the last six words of the *Gettysburg Address*? (2)

34. What was the nickname of Ivan IV of Russia? (1)

35. Name 23 helping verbs. (2)

36. From whom did the cardigan sweater get its name? (1)

37. Use *their, they're* and *there* correctly in a single sentence. (1)

38. What is _____'s middle name? (3)

39. To what period of American history does Button Gwinnett belong? (2)

40. What kind of food is *headcheese*? (1)

41. What do honey bees collect? (1)

42. Write down 20 words that rhyme with *plan.* *(4)*

43. What are lead pencils made of? (1)

44. What metal is the nickel coin primarily composed of? (1)

45. Who was the 22nd president of the United States? (2)

46. There are 12 buttons on a touch-tone telephone. What letters are on the button with the number 7? (1)

47. Write down the names of 15 Christmas carols. (2)

48. Who wrote *Great Expectations*? (1)

49. Have your whole group sing "Rudolph the Red-Nosed Reindeer" to the class. Have your runner tell your teacher when you are ready. You must sing the whole song. Everyone must sing. Only the first group to do this correctly will receive tokens. (5)

50. Write a dependent clause. (1)

51. List five synonyms for the word *beautiful.* (1)

52. Fill in the blank correctly at the end of this sequence: 3, 9, 81, _____. (2)

53. Personify a snowflake in one sentence. (2)

54. What are five useful things you might do with a used, dry Christmas tree? (2)

55. Write down 10 clichés. (3)

56. Who was the women's U.S. figure skating champion of 1964? (2)

57. Who wrote the poem "The Raven"? (1)

58. Name the five Great Lakes. (1)

59. Name the horse that won the Kentucky Derby in 1981. (2)

60. When is _____'s birthday? (2)

Answer Key
Holiday Challenge

1. A kangaroo
2. Answers will vary.
3. James Thurber
4. Leo
5. Dasher, Dancer, Prancer, Vixen, Comet, Cupid, Donner, Blitzen
6. Pittsburgh Steelers
7. Answers will vary.
8. 13
9. Verona, Italy
10. Potomac
11. Holiday style
12.–17. Answers will vary.
18. Any one of the following: *Genesis, Exodus, Leviticus, Numbers, Deuteronomy, Joshua, Judges, Ruth, Samuel, Kings, Chronicles, Ezra, Nehemiah, Esther, Job, Psalms, Proverbs, Ecclesiastes, Song of Solomon, Isaiah, Jeremiah, Lamentations, Ezekiel, Daniel, Hosea, Joel, Amos, Obadiah, Jonah, Micah, Nathan, Habakkuk, Zephaniah, Haggai, Zechariah, Malachi*
19. Nouns, verbs, adjectives, adverbs, prepositions, interjections, conjunctions, pronouns
20. Eight days
21.–22. Answers will vary.
23. Muhammed Ali
24. better, best
25. Answers will vary.
26. Russia
27.–29. Answers will vary.
30. a snowman / Parson Brown
31. Any one the following: *Love's Labour's Lost; The Comedy of Errors; The Two Gentlemen of Verona; A Midsummer Night's Dream; The Merchant of Venice; The Taming of the Shrew; The Merry Wives of Windsor; Much Ado About Nothing; As You Like It; Twelfth Night; All's Well That Ends Well;*
Measure for Measure; Pericles; Cymbeline; The Winter's Tale; The Tempest; King John; Richard II; Henry IV, Parts I and II; Henry V; Henry VI, Parts I, II and III; Richard III; Henry VIII; Titus Andronicus; Romeo and Juliet; Julius Caesar; Hamlet; Troilus and Cressida; Othella; King Lear; Macbeth; Antony and Cleopatra; Timon of Athens; Coriolanus
32. 3.9
33. Shall not perish from the earth.
34. Ivan the Terrible
35. Is, be, am, are, was, were, been, has, have, had, do, does, did, can, could, shall, should, will, would, may, might, must, been, being
36. James Thomas Brudnell, 7th Earl of Cardigan
37.–38. Answers will vary.
39. Revolutionary War
40. A jellied loaf or sausage containing chopped and boiled animal parts
41. Nectar
42. Answers will vary.
43. Graphite
44. Copper
45. Grover Cleveland
46. PRS
47. Answers will vary.
48. Charles Dickens
49.–51. Answers will vary.
52. 6561
53.–55. Answers will vary.
56. Peggy Fleming
57. Edgar Allen Poe
58. Erie, Huron, Michigan, Ontario, Superior
59. Secretariat
60. Answers will vary.

Crazy Sentences

This game often inspires even the most reluctant writers. It is absorbing, encourages creativity and gives students practice writing, all at the same time. You can also vary the game in many ways.

Materials

Just a chalkboard and chalk, as well as paper for everyone.

Instructions

The first time you play the game, spend a bit of time reviewing nouns. Talk about the difference between interesting, specific nouns and vague, general nouns. For example, you might give the students the noun *shoe* and ask them to come up with a more specific noun that means the same thing — like *sandals, heels* or *sneakers*. Then have them add modifiers to make the noun even more specific — like *ragged, high-topped sneakers with neon pink shoelaces*.

Then have everyone think of a topic for a sentence. The topic should be in the form of an interesting noun, with modifiers. When everyone is ready, choose three students to share their topics. Write these topics on the board.

Explain that each student is now to take all three topics on the board and write one complete sentence that includes all of them — and that makes sense.

Have students share their results. Then try building up, seeing if students can write a sentence including four topics, then five, etc.

Variations

• Have students write their topics on slips of paper. Collect them and put them in a jar. Draw slips for the first sentence and save the rest for other days, until all topics are used.

• So that more topics are used, assign a different set to each row of students.

• Choose ten or more topics and have students write paragraphs instead of sentences.

• Type up all of the topics the students have written. Then have each student try to include all of them in a short story. This is a real challenge!

Suggestions

• Have students write new topics after you have tried the game once. Because the students will then understand the game, the new topics will usually be much more interesting.

• Encourage students to write down some intangible topics occasionally, like *love* or *honesty*.

• Have fun with this. Let volunteers read their sentences aloud. Or have the students turn in their sentences; then select interesting or clever ones to share with the class later. Don't be afraid to try a set of topics yourself and share your results.

Rhyming Conversation

Try writing a rhyming conversation between Pam and Sam. Here's how it works:

After the first person speaks, each person then says two sentences. The first sentence must end in a word that rhymes with the last word of the previous sentence. The second sentence starts a new rhyme.

That sounds complicated, but it's not nearly as difficult as it sounds, once you get started. Here's an example of a rhyming conversation:

SAM: Pam, I'd like to take you on a date.

PAM: I can't wait!
     Can we go to the show?

SAM: No, no.
     I'd like to go play tennis.

PAM: But I'd much rather do that with Dennis.
     Why don't we go out for a burger and fries?

SAM: No, I think I'd rather do that with the guys.
     Why don't we go to the dance?

PAM: Not a chance.
     I'm going to that with Mike.

SAM: I've got the best idea then: Take a hike!

Now you try it, using your own paper to write out the conversation.

PAM: Have you studied for the test?

SAM: (He first says something that rhymes with *test*.
     Then he starts a new rhyme.)

PAM: (She first says something that rhymes with the last word in Sam's last line, above.
     Then she starts a new rhyme.)

Now continue the conversation on your own.

Answer Key
Rhyming Conversation

Answers will vary. Here is one possibility.

PAM: Have you studied for the test?

SAM: Yes, but I didn't do my best.
I kept being bothered by my cat.

PAM: A kitten — I remember that.
Is she really grown now?

SAM: Yes, she's eating like a cow.
Did you do your paper for history?

PAM: Yes, but where I put it is a mystery.
It's something I really need to find.

SAM: If you'd find one for me I wouldn't mind.
I can't think of anything to write about.

PAM: I wrote about the history of the girl scout.
But I guess I'll have to do it again.

SAM: I'll see you tomorrow around ten.

Space Race

This game is a good one to use when the students have earned a treat or when they need something active to do. It demonstrates the importance of clear communication.

Materials

- A blindfold.
- 5–8 "obstacles" (chairs, desks, stools, students themselves — anything easily moved).

Organization

Move all the desks to the sides of the classroom, leaving a large open area in the middle of the room. Be sure to leave a wall at one end of the room open as well. Divide the class into two teams and have the teams sit on each side of the open space.

Instructions

Explain that the open area of the room represents outer space and that the open wall represents a space station. Each team's task is to try to direct a spaceship to a safe landing at the space station.

However, there are a few problems. First, the spaceship pilot is unable to see because the lights on the spaceship have gone out. Second, the radio is on the blink and only works one way. That means the pilot can hear instructions from the space station control tower but can't speak back. Third, there are meteors, satellites and comets for the pilot to avoid while approaching the space station.

Flip a coin to see which team is to get the first chance to land a spaceship. The winning team selects one person to be the first pilot, and that pilot is blindfolded.

The opposite team places obstacles in space, making sure that it is indeed possible to walk around and between those obstacles without bumping into them.

The pilot's team then begins giving instructions. Each team member may speak one sentence only, giving the pilot instructions for proceeding toward the space station without bumping into an obstacle. If the pilot touches an obstacle, the spaceship has crashed. If that happens, the opposing team members choose a new pilot and take their turn at trying to direct a safe landing.

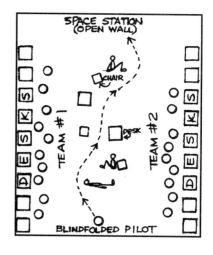

A pilot lands safely when he or she travels past all the obstacles, without crashing, and touches the wall at the opposite end of the runway. A successful landing earns a team one point. Of course, the team with the most points at the end of the game wins.

Suggestions

- It is fun to use students as obstacles, thus getting more students actively involved in the game at once. For example, a student might lie down, hands over head, to create a long obstacle. Or the student might stand, one arm extended, so that the pilot would have to be directed to go under the arm.

- It is important to insist on safety. When the pilot is about to reach the opposite wall, be sure the students instruct that person to extend his or hands in front of him and proceed slowly. Similarly, be sure to intervene if any student gives an instruction that might be potentially dangerous — such as taking a step onto a person's hand or foot.

- Be sure that the students understand that a pilot should not move until the person giving directions has completed his or her sentence. Once the pilot moves, the person cannot continue with the sentence. This helps to avoid instructions like, "Take two steps to the left — no bigger steps — and then get down on your hands and knees — no, not yet." Students will have to think through their instructions before they begin speaking.

- Don't worry if the first few spaceships crash into obstacles right away. The students will quickly learn that, to be successful, their instructions must be precise.

Saying What You Mean

This game is a good introduction to a unit on giving and following directions. The game is interesting for students and, at the same time, helps them to see the importance of clear, precise wording.

Materials

- Copies of the direction cards that follow, cut apart and mounted on dark paper so that the lines don't show through the back. (You will need one card for every two students in your class.)

- At least one piece of white paper or notebook paper, per student.

- Pencils or markers.

Organization

Assign each student a partner, or let students choose their own partners. Have each set of partners turn their desks so that they face one another.

Instructions

Give one student in each pair a directions card, cautioning the students to hold the cards so that their partners don't see the figures on them.

Tell the students with cards that it is their task to give careful, complete instructions for drawing the figure on the card that each holds. The students without cards are to follow their partners' instructions, trying to reproduce the unseen figures.

Stress that everyone must follow these guidelines:

- Only the person giving directions may speak.

- The person drawing may not ask questions but must do the best he or she can to follow the directions, as given.

- The person drawing should hold his or her paper so that the person giving instructions cannot see it.

When everyone is finished, have students share their work, holding up the original cards beside the final drawings. Many or most drawings will not even resemble the originals and should cause a lot of laughter.

Talk about the importance of being specific and clear in giving directions. Discuss what students might have done to make their directions clearer. Then have students try the exercise again, with partners switching places and trading for new cards. The second set of drawings should be much more accurate than the first.

Suggestions

- A good follow-up activity is to follow the same procedure described above, but having the students write their instructions instead of giving them orally. The following day each student can try to follow someone else's written instructions.

- Another good follow-up activity is to draw a simple picture of a house on the board. Have the students see how many of them can write effective directions for drawing the house. Test the directions by following them, at the board, the next day. Have one student read while you do exactly as instructed, making sure to do the wrong thing when directions are ambiguous or unclear.

- One more interesting activity is to have the students try to give you directions for tying a shoe. Place a shoe on a stool or desk in front of the class, where all can see it clearly. Have volunteers tell you, one at a time, what to do. Be sure to play "dumb," doing exactly as they say. Eventually, the students should see that they must think about what they are going to say, choosing their words carefully to achieve the intended results.

Direction Cards for "Saying What You Mean"

The pages that follow can be photocopied to make the direction cards necessary for the activity "Saying What You Mean."

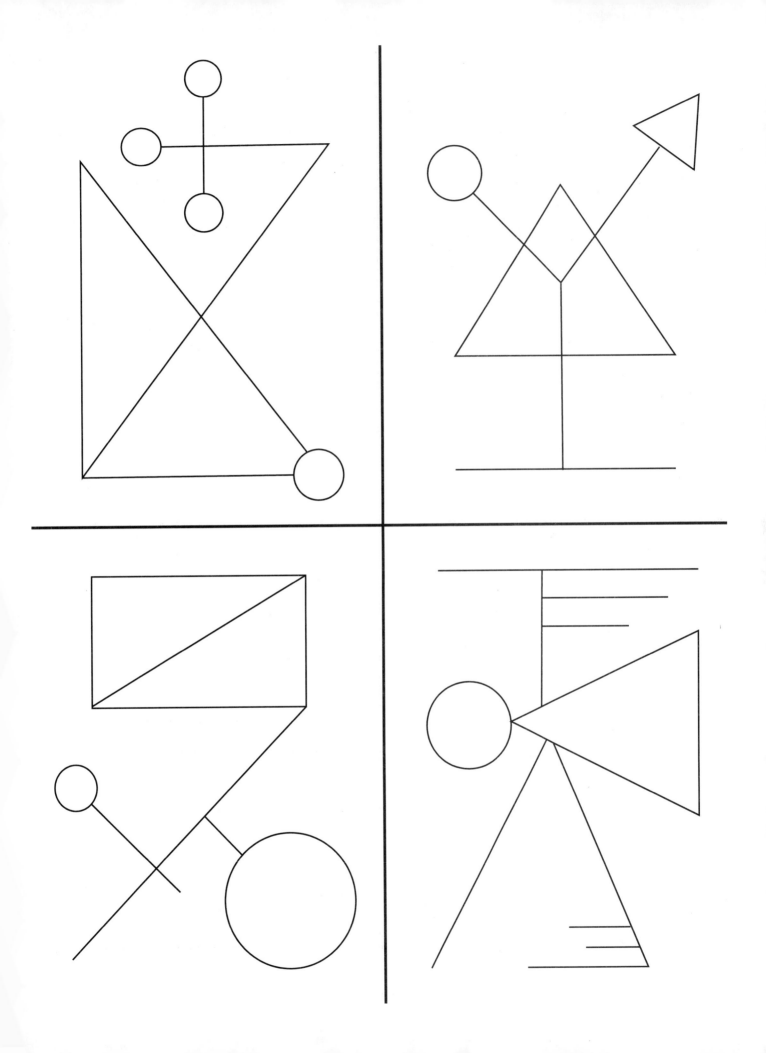

To Order More Copies of
Surviving Last Period on Fridays
and Other Desperate Situations

Please send me _____ copies of Surviving Last Period on Fridays and Other Desperate Situations. I am enclosing $15.95, plus shipping and handling ($4.00 for one book, $1.00 for each additional book). Colorado residents add 46¢ sales tax per book. Total amount $_____.

Name   _____

(School) _____
(Include only if using school address.)

Address _____

City _____ State _____ Zip Code _____

Phone _____

Method of Payment:

    ❑ Payment enclosed   ❑ Visa/MC/Discover   ❑ Purchase Order (Please attach.)

Credit Card# _____Expiration Date _____

Signature _____

Cardholder Name:

Cardholder Billing Address: (if different from shipping address)

Address _____

City _____ State _____ Zip Code _____

Send to:

Cottonwood Press, Inc.
109-B Cameron Drive
Fort Collins, CO 80525
1-800-864-4297

www.cottonwoodpress.com

**Call for a free catalog of practical materials for
English and language arts teachers, grades 5-12.**